Three One Act
Children's Bible Plays

Tell The Truth

Jesus In The Temple

Pray

by
Sue L. Adkins

Sue L. Adkins

Three One Act
Children Bible Plays

Cheudi Publishing Plano, Texas 75094

ROYALITY NOTE

The possession of this book (e-book or hard copy), without a written authorization first having been obtained from the publisher, confers no right or license, to professionals or amateurs, to produce the play, publicly or in private, for gain or charity. However, productions of this play are encouraged, and those who wish to present it may secure the necessary permission from Cheudi Publishing, Plano, Texas 75094, USA.

Professional producers are requested to apply to Cheudi Publishing for Royalty quotation.

This play may be presented by amateurs, upon payment to Cheudi Publishing of a royalty (to be determined) for each performance, one week before the date the play is to be given. The play is fully protected by copyright, and anyone presenting the play without the consent of Cheudi Publishing, will be liable to penalties provided by the copyright law.

Each time the play is produced, the name of the author must be carried in all publicity, advertising, fliers, and programmes.

Sue L. Adkins

TABLE OF PLAYS

Sue L. Adkins

Tell
the
Truth

Is that the truth?

Tell the Truth
by Sue L. Adkins
Music and Lyrics by Sue L. Adkins

Jesus Heals a Man Born Blind *John 9:1*

Brady Bible Bumble Bee: (*Enters*) "Where is it? There's something. Let me think!" (*Thinks*) "Humm...! What is it? What? I just can't remember!" (*Notices audience*) "Oh! Hi! I'm Brady! Brady Bible Bumble Bee! I just was trying to think of something. But I forgot." (*Thinks, Shrugs*) "Oh well. I'll get it! But until I do, why don't we sing? Okay? Yes. That might help me remember. Will you sing with me?" (*Waits for a response*) "Good! What? You don't know the song? Oh-h! Don't worry. It's easy! I'll teach you. First listen! Then sing with me! Okay? Good. Here we go!"

Song: Let's Learn

Brady: (*Hears noise off stage, is startled*) "What was that!" (*To the audience*) "Did you hear it? Me too!" (*Notices a rope on the floor leading offstage*) "Look!" (Pointing) "How did that rope get there? (*Shrugs*) "Should I? (*Nods*) "Yes! I'll pull it and see what happens. What do you think?" (Children respond.) "Okay!" (*Puts his finger to his lips*) "Sh-

7

h-h!" (*Tiptoes up to the rope*) "I'll just, reach down, and grab!" (*Rope is jerked away. He gasps*) "What happened?" (*Thinks*) "Should I try again?" (*Children respond*) "Okay! (*Whispers*) "Here goes…!" (*Rope is pulled away again*) "Oh!" (*Gets idea; Pretends to button his lips, tiptoes toward rope again, reaches for it as rope is pulled away. Goes toward it again, whistling; sneaks up, steps on it, smiles, grabs rope, and pulls it towards him, looks at attached sign*) "Oh! Yes! That's it! I need to give you the Word for today!" (*Clears his throat*) "THE WORD FOR TODAY IS: (*Pause*) "TRUTH! Now I know what I needed to remember to "Tell the TRUTH!" (*Points to the sign*) "Jesus always told the truth! He did right! And He did not lie!"

Song: Tell the Truth
(Brady and Children Sing)

Brady: (*To audience*) "Our story today is about a blind man. He sits in front of the Temple everyday and begged for whatever help he can get. One day there was a big commotion. He heard people talking. A man had come into the city, and he was healing people. That means He was making sick people well." Sh-h-h-h! Pay close attention! We'll close our lips and use our ears to listen as the story is told. It happened in the City of Jerusalem. Let's listen!" (*Brady exits*)

Scene I
Jerusalem

(Neighbor leads blind man in and helps him as he sits down to beg in front of the Temple. Neighbor exits.)

Man: "I've seen it myself! He touched a man who was lame, and that man picked up his bed and walked."

Man II: "That cannot be true! A magician's trick! I've seen it many times before."

Man I: "No! It was no trick! I was there! This man tells the truth! That one has special powers not seen or done by anyone before!"

Blind Man: *(To the men)* "But who is this One you speak about?"

Man II: *(Irritated)* "No concern to you!"

Blind Man: "I mean no harm. I only ask the name of this "Great Healer."

Man I: "What can it matter that he knows the name?"

(*To Blind Man*) "Jesus! That is what others call him!"

Blind Man: (*To himself*) "Jesus." (*Players freeze*)

Brady Bumble Bee: (*Enters*) "The blind man thought and thought about how he could meet the 'One' called Jesus." (To Children) "When you want something what do you do? Who do you ask?" (*Children Answer*) "If you want ice cream, new clothes or a game, who do you ask?" (*Children answer*) "That's right! You ask your mom or dad, a grown-up. There was something the blind man wanted too! He couldn't see like me and you! He heard men talking about a "Healer," the One who made people well. He must have thought that maybe this one could make him see.' For many years he sat in the same spot day after day. It was hard for him to get from place to place. He couldn't go to look for the Healer. Everyday he sat and asked for food, tokens, and took whatever people gave him. Would this Healer ever come his way he must have wondered? Then one day there was a big commotion, and loud talk. People rushed by him."

(Noisy shouting and p*eople enter rushing by*)

Man I: "The Healer!"

Man II: "IT IS! Jesus is coming this way! Make way! Make way for the 'Healer!' He comes!"

11

Brady Bible Bumble Bee: (*To Children*) "There was pushing and loud shouts of joy and excitement. Let's watch and see what happens."

Blind Man: "Healer? Do my ears hear right? Can it be?"

Brady Bible Bumble Bee: "He reaches out and tries to stop anyone he can. He had to get somebody's attention."

Blind Man: "Who is coming? Tell me!"

Brady Bible Bumble Bee: "He stops somebody and asks."

Blind Man: "Who did you say? Who comes this way? The Healer, did you say?"

Man III: "It is! The very One! He comes this way! Yes! The Healer! Jesus! I'm told he has *great power* and that He works many miracles!" (*Characters freeze*)

Brady Bible Bumble Bee: (*To children*) "The Blind man was happy." And he *thinks:* 'Oh, if this is the great Healer then he must find a way to get Him to stop and help him.' (*Jesus and the Disciple enter. As they walked along the path the Disciple see the man blind from birth. They stop near him and ask Jesus a question*)

Disciple: (*Sees the blind man*) "Master! Tell us! Who sinned! Was it this man or his parents so that he was born blind?"

Jesus: (*Looks over at him*) "This man did not sin and neither did his parents. He is blind so that God's wonderful work can be seen in his life. While I am here I will do God's work. While I am in the world, I am the light of the world." (*Jesus goes over to the blind man. He spits on the ground, bends and stirs to mix it with dirt. He scoops some up in his hand and puts it on the blind man's eyes*)

Man I: "Look! He spits on the ground, makes mud, and now puts it on the blind man's eyes!"

Man II: "What is the meaning of this?" (*Confused*)

Brady: (*To children*) "Have you ever made mud-cakes?" (*Children Respond*) "Why did Jesus do that? He put mud on the Blind Man's eyes? Hmmm, let's see what happens!"

Jesus: "Go to the water, the Pool of Siloam. Wash the mud from your eyes and you will see."

Blind man: (*Men help him over to the water. He washes his eyes; Opens them one at a time; Blinks* *and rubs his eyes. Realizes he can see. (Excited)* "I can see! I see your face, sky, and my hands." *(Hears something and looks up and all around)* "Birds! Hills! (Laughs and Twirls around; Runs about. Another man enters. Notices blind man)* "I can see...! You! And You! All of You, and EVERYTHING!" *(Hugs everyone, then drops to his knees and cries with joy)*

Neighbor: (Enters *and observers the once blind man)* "Can that be the same man I bring to sit at the Temple and beg?"

Man III:　　　"Yes! He is the same one."

Neighbor:　　(To Blind Man) "How is it that you can see?" *(Blind man is crying, but joyous)* "Is it true? How did this happen?"

Blind Man: "The Healer! The One called Jesus took mud and put it on my eyes!" *(Crying, excited and happy)* "He told me to go to the pool! The water of Siloam! He commanded me to wash and I would be..."

Neighbor: *(Interrupts)* "What? What do you say? Impossible!"

Man II: "He speaks the truth! He did what Jesus told him!"

Man I: "It is so! I saw it myself.

Neighbor: (*Goes over to the once Blind man and stops him*) "It must be a trick or some Witch craft!"

Blind Man: "No! Look at me! All of it is true! I did as Jesus told me! I went to the pool and washed away the mud He put on my eyes! And just as He said! I can see! Jesus told me the truth! I was blind but now I can see!" (*Cries out with joy*)

Neighbor: "Crazy!" (Look around at them) "All of you are crazy!"

(All *Exits*)

Brady: (*To Children*) "Was the Blind man crazy?" (*Children Respond, "No!"*)

Brady: "That's right! Jesus healed the Blind Man. Didn't he?"

Children: "Yes!"

Brady: "He spit in the dirt and made mud and put the mud on the Blind man's eyes. Then what happened?" (*Children respond*)

Brady: "That's right! He told him to go to the water and do what?" (*Children respond*) "Yes! Wash the mud off! And what happened?" Children respond) "He did what Jesus said and he could see!"

Brady: "Good! Give me a "T! (*He holds up each letter as he call them)* You say it!" (*Children respond "T!"*) Give me an "R!" (*"R!"*) Give me a "U!" (*"U!"*) Give me a "T!" (*"T!"*) Give me an "H!" (*"H!"*). What does it spell? (*Holds sign: Truth; Children respond "Truth!"*) "A little louder!" (Children Respond: "Truth!") "I can't hear you!" (*Children Respond: "Truth!"*) "Jesus told the what?" (Children Respond: "Truth!") "Say it again!" (*Children Respond: "Truth!"*) "That's right! And that's what we must do! Good! Now let's sing the song about Truth!"

Song: Tell The Truth
(Brady Sing)

Brady: "That's our story!" (*Brady asks a question*) "We must tell the what?" (*Children respond: "Truth!"*)

Brady: "That's right! The Truth! Now let's sing the "Let's Learn" song again."
Song: (All Sing) Let's Learn

(END)

Jesus In The Temple

By Sue L. Adkins
Music and Lyrics by Sue L. Adkins

Act I
Scene I

(Brady Bible Bumble Bee enters)

Brady B. B. Bee: "Hi everybody! I'm Brady! Brady Bible Bumble Bee! And I'm glad you came to visit me! We're going to have fun and learn about something we all must do! But first, do you remember our theme song? Okay! I'll start and sing it through once. Then you join in and sing too. Remember? It's called: "Let's learn!""

Song: Let's Learn

(Brady and Children Sing)Brady: "That was good! Do you know that God wants all children to obey their parents? When you obey it shows that you love them. I love my parents and I love God, but sometimes it's hard for me to obey. But it makes God happy when we do. Jesus obeyed his parents and showed us how to live good lives! He wants us to be good and to please God."

Song: Obey
(Brady Sings)

Brady: "Terrific! Any time you hear the word "Obey" in our story a bell will ring!" (*Bell rings*) "Like that! Ok?" (*Children respond*) "Great!" (*Searches large bag*) "I brought something. It's in here somewhere. Here it is! *(Finds his Big Binoculars)* My binoculars! Let's look through our binoculars and see what Jesus said and did." (*Notices children don't have them*) "What? You didn't bring your binoculars?" (*Puts binoculars down*) "Hmmm… Oh that's all right! Let's see what we can do." (*Gets idea*) "I know! Why don't we use our "hand binoculars?" You know! We all have them! Take your hands and curve your fingers around to your thumbs, just like this! Leave an opening! Big O's on both hands! That's it! Great! Now put them together! You've got it! Yes! That's how you make hand binoculars! Now we'll put them up to our eyes and see what we can see!" (*Boy enters runs and kicks at stick*) "Good! Hmmm…! Over there! I see him now! Do you see? Look! Let's see what happens!"

Scene II

Joseph: (*Joseph and wife enters. Shades eyes; Looks for his son*)
Joseph: (*Calls son*) "Boy! Jesus!"

Joseph: (*To his wife*) "Look how our son grows. He gets bigger every day."

Mother: "Yes. And his thoughts are much beyond his years."

Jesus: "Yes Sir! I'm coming!" (*Waves; Runs home*)

Jesus: "Here I am father!"

Joseph: "Son, we leave early tomorrow morning before dawn. We join the other families and journey to Jerusalem for the feast of the Passover. Finish your work! Wood needs stacking and animals must be fed!"

Jesus: "Yes father!" (*Gathers twigs; his friend Bieleum enters and watches Jesus work, teases, pushes, tries to get him to stop and play*) "I have work Bieleum! (*Bieleum continues teasing*)

Parent: (*His father calls*) "Bieleum!"

Bieleum: "Yes, Father!" (*To Jesus*) "I must go! When we return from Passover we should go to the sand-dunes and play."

Jesus: "No! Not there! We are told to stay away!"

Bieleum: "Who will know?"

Jesus: "We will know Bieleum!"

Bieleum: That is so. But who will know besides you and me?"

Jesus: "I won't go! We are told to stay away!"

Bieleum: (Teasing) "Jesus is scared! I will know, and you will know. And no one else"

Jesus: "We have to do what our parents tell us to do! We must obey!" (Bell r*ings! Characters freeze*)

(EXIT)

Bumble Bee: (*To Children*) "That was our bell! Did you hear it? Jesus' friend Bieleum wants to do something wrong! What do you say when somebody wants you to disobey?" (*Waits for response*) "That's right! You say No! You tell them: That's not right! That's wrong!" (*Makes a sad face*) "We all need to think!" (*Points to his head*) "Think before you speak! Because," (*puts hand to ear for response*) "We Should Obey!" (*Bell rings*) "There's our word! What is it?" (*Children respond "Obey!" Bell rings*) "Good!"

Song: You Must Obey
(Brady Sings)

Bumble Bee: "That's right! Now let's see more of our story." (*Vendors enter and setup wares. Travelers enter, look at displays*) "Jesus and his family are in the city now. Do you like to go to the city? How do you get to the city near you, by airplane?" (*Makes sound of airplane; holds his arms out and moves as if flying*) "Come on! Hold your arms out like wings! Now make the sound of an airplane flying! Buzz! Buzz! What about in a boat?" (*Reaches up and pretends to pull a cord; makes sound of boat whistle*) "Yes! You do it too! Rock and bob like you're on a boat! Now pull the cord and make the sound of the boat whistle! Is that how Jesus and his family got to the city?"

Children Respond: "No!"

Bumble Bee: "You're right! Big groups of people from all over the town walked and some even rode donkeys. Hee-Haw! Now let's see what happened to Jesus and his family!"

(*Mother, Joseph and other travelers enter marketplace; look at displays*)

Mother: "I love coming to the city for Passover. There is much to do and see!"

Joseph: "Yes! Many have made the journey! We must stay together! (*Mother nods in agreement. Jesus looks all around; wanders around looking at all the wares. Points, Stops, Stares, at the jugglers, fire eater, and snake charmer. Mother stops to look, touch cloth and ask about wares, Father laughs and talks to other men. All get distracted, family gets separated, go in different directions. Mother and Father talk, visit with other families, some barter for goods. The group is joyous. They gather then head out for home. Mary and Joseph think Jesus is following along with all the other children. After walking a while they realize that Jesus is not with the group. Begin to search, stop and ask other travelers for help, and call for him"* (***Author's note: This can be done as a choreographed piece***). "Jesus! Jesus!"

Mother: (*To other travelers*) "Have you seen Jesus, my son?" (*Shakes head no*) "Our son, have you seen him? (*Shakes heads no. She calls out for him*) "Jesus! (*Looks around*) "Where could he be?"

Joseph: (*To fellow travelers*) "Have you seen our son?" (*Traveler shakes head, no*) "I fear he is left back in Jerusalem! We must hurry, return, and find him!" (*Gestures to others, they are going back to the city. Hugs friends, waves goodbye, turns and heads back to the city*)

Mother: (*Crying*) "Oh Joseph! I pray he is safe!"

Joseph: (Hugs her) "We will find him!"
(All Exit)

23

Brady: (*To Children*) "Where could he be? Have you seen him? Let me think!" (*Jumps up, put his finger to his head. Thinks of something, changes his mind, shakes his head*) "No! That's not it! I need help!" (*To Children*) "Can you help me?" (*Children respond*) "If I could just remember what happened when Jesus got separated from his parents. Hmm! Maybe he's standing there looking at the jugglers!" (*Makes juggling motion*) "Do you think that's where he is?" (*Children answer*) "No? Yes?" (*Children answer*) "Maybe he went back home? What do you think? No?" (*He cups his hand under his chin and thinks again*) "Could He be at the dunes with His friend?" (*Children should answer no*) "No. He wouldn't go there. Would he?" (*Children answer "no"*) "He was told not to. And he told his friend Bieleum he wouldn't go, because Jesus obeys!" (*Bell rings; He Laughs*) "What does Jesus do?" (*Brady and the Children answer*) "He obeys!" (*Bell rings again. "I knew that! "But where did He go? He's not with his parents. They looked everywhere. It's getting late and they need to get back home. Hmmm! Where is that Big Book? You know the one to look in and find out what happens? Where did I put it?" (*Looks around and discovers it*) "Oh! There it is!" (*Picks up huge book with the word, BIBLE, in big bold letters*)

Song: The Bible (Brady Sings)

Bumble Bee: (*Turns pages*) "Now! Let's see what it says!" (*Tries to read; Squints; Realizes he's not wearing his glasses; Searches his bag; Pulls out a large pair of glasses. Puts them on; smiles; turns the pages in the Big Bible*) "Here it is!" (*Reads silently*) "Hmm! Okay!" (*Puts a large marker in Bible and closes it*) "Now I know where He is!" (*To Children*) "So! Let's open our eyes real wide," (*Points to eyes*) "And listen with our ears" (*Points to ears*) "real close to hear what's said." (*He opens to passage again and reads aloud*).

BBB: "Here it is." (*Reads*) "His parents looked for him. It was three Days' before they found him in the 'Temple'. There he was Listening and Talking with the Teachers; Asking and Answering Questions. They were amazed that He understood what they were talking about and how "Smart" He was in answering their questions. Let's watch and listen!"

(*Outside the Temple, they stop and ask people for help*)
Mother: "There is talk of some young boy in the Temple!"

Joseph: "The Temple? But why would he be there?" (*Mother shrugs*) "Let's hurry!" (*Exit)*)

(*In the Temple, Jesus and the Teachers are talking. He is surrounded by them*)

Jesus: "How can we recognize God's goodness?"

Teachers I: "God gives power to the King to Rule over all the people and give them what they need."

Jesus: "The Sun shines and the rain falls over all the land and all the people," (*Joseph and mother enter. Look all around. See boy surrounded by Teachers.*)) "...and over the King and every man. Goodness and the things of God serve all."

Teacher II: "We recognize the goodness in God because God chose us to rule over the people. Jesus: "Is not God's goodness given to all? For we have but to look,"

(*Mother rushes over to him*)

Mother: (*Hugs him*) "Son! Jesus! We have been worried and searched everywhere for you!"

Joseph: "You strayed! And separated from the group!"

Jesus: "There was no need to look for me? Did you not know that I must be about my Father's business?"

Joseph: (*Joseph and Mary look at each other and seem confused*) "Come son!

We must leave!" (*To Teacher*) "Thank you! We are grateful to you for talking with our son, and for answering his questions."

Teacher III: "We had questions for him as well!" (*Joseph and Mother excuse themselves from the gathering*)

Joseph: (*Mother and Jesus*) "We can not catch up to the others. They are more than a day's journey ahead. But if we hurry we can be home soon behind them."

(All *Exit*)

Bumble Bee: (*To Children*) "What did Jesus do?" (*Waits for response*) "I can't hear you!" (*Children respond*) "What did He do?" (*Children respond*) "That's right! Jesus obeyed his parents." (*Bell Rings*) "He stopped talking and excused himself from the teachers right then and there and left with his parents for home." (*Smiles*) "That was a good lesson wasn't it? And just like Jesus did, we can show love for our parents and for God when we do what?"

Children: "OBEY" (*Bell Rings*)

Bumble Bee: "Yes! Obey!" (*Bell Rings again*) "Let's sing our song again. Do you remember it? Good! Here we go!"

Song: You Must Obey
(Brady Sings)

(END)

Pray

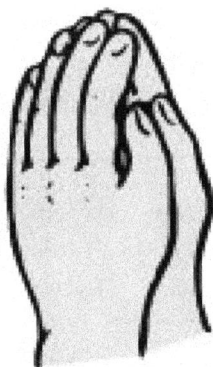

By Sue L. Adkins

Music and Lyric by Sue L. Adkins

Act I
Scene I

Brady Bible Bumble Bee: (*Enters. Looking for something... Notices children*) "Oh! Hi! It's me again! Brady, Brady Bible Bumble Bee!" (*Waves*) "You know what we're going to do! Don't you? Yes! That's right! Let's sing our song. You remember! Of course you do? It's called "Let's Learn! All right! Let's go!"

Song: Let's Learn
(Brady and Children Sing)

BBB: (*Looking around*) "I was just looking for something. Where can it be? Do you know?" (*Children respond*) "You don't? Well, let me think. Let's see!" (*Goes over his morning activities and pantomimes each one*) "First: I washed my face this morning! And brushed my teeth! Combed my fuzzy locks! Now let me think!" (*Pause*) "That's strange! I always have such a good memory. Oh well! I'd better eat my breakfast" (*Sits down and lifts a large bowl of sunflower soup. Gets a big spoon; Remembers*) "Now I know what I was trying to remember! To Pray! Yes! Pray! That's it! That's our word for today!" (*Pulls out a large placard, the word "PRAY" is printed on it*) "Here it

is: PRAY!" (*To Children*) "Say it with," (*Pause*)
"Wait!
Let's count to three and say it together!
Ready?" (*Children respond*) "One! Two!
Three!" (*All: "PRAY!"*) "Good! We All Should
Pray!"

Song: "What Do You Do When You Pray"

(Brady Sings)

Brady: (*To Children*) "God tells us to pray! It's how
we say 'Thank You, to Him! You say thank you to
your brothers and sisters when they help you do
things, don't you? When they share their chips, or
help you pick up your toys. What about when they
give you a bite of sandwich? (Children may respond)
"Do you say thank you?" (*Children respond*)
"Good! Do you say 'thank-you' when somebody is
nice to you?" (*Children respond*) "That's good too!"
Do you know that you can thank God too? (*Children
respond*) "Yes! You can thank him for your family
and friends," (*Add up the number of times on fingers*)
"And for the food you have to eat. For Everything!
And when you do something wrong you can tell God
that you're sorry. He will forgive you! That's right!
He will!" (*Telephone rings*) "My phone is ringing. I
wonder whose calling. Excuse me. I'd better answer
it." (*Looks in bag, pulls out phone and answers*)
"Hello. Oh! Hi Jessie," (*To Children*) "It's my
friend Jessie. Yes! There is? All right! I'll get it!

Thank you! Thanks for calling, Jessie. Goodbye!" (*Puts phone back in bag; To Children*) "Jessie said he left something on the porch for me. I wonder what it is. I'd better go out and get it! ...be right back! Wait here." (*Exits; Returns with wrapped present*) "It's a present! I like to get presents. Don't you?" (*Shakes box*) Better open it and see what's inside! (*Pulls out a note*) "Wander what it says? Do you want to know? I do too! Let's open it and see! (*Opens note*) "It's a question! I'll read it out loud! It says: 'When You Pray, What Do You Do?" (*Repeats it, slow deliberate)*) "When you pray, what do you do? Let me think. Did you know that Jesus prayed? And He explains how we can pray too! We don't have to say the words He said. We can say our own words. We don't have to pray a certain way or at a certain time. We don't even have to turn a certain way or stand or sit. We can have our eyes opened or closed. We can bow our heads or not. And we can just say what's in our heart. Talk to God in your own way. But because we want to please God we should speak to Him with love and respect."

(*Jesus and Disciples Enter*)

Brady: "Yes! Jesus was a wonderful teacher. Do some of you want to be teachers when you grow up?" (*Children respond*) "Good! You'll be *great* teachers! Jesus taught his disciples to pray, but He didn't say that they had to say the exact words He said. They could use their own words!" (*Others enter*) "Jesus taught us about prayer. Look! Here we can see Him as He teaches His Disciples."

Scene II

(Jesus talks to His disciples. Matthew 6:5-15)

Jesus: "You should pray in the quiet of your heart. Don't pray before a group to get attention. Say what you have to say! You don't have to talk on and on!"

Disciples: "Yes, Master."

Jesus: "God knows what you need even before you ask. Forgive others when they are mean to you and God will forgive you when you need Him too!" (*Exit*)

BBB: (*To Children*) "Jesus helped his Disciples by telling them to pray, but He also showed them because He prayed too. Here's a song that talks about prayer."

Song: "When You Pray" (Brady Sings)

Brady: (*Knock at the door*) "Did you hear something? I did too!" (*Hears the knock again*) "There's someone at the door! Let's see who it is!" (*Goes to the door, lets guest in*) "Hi Babs!

Babs Butterfly: "Hello Brady!"

BBB: "Come in!" (*To Children*) "It's Babs!"

Babs: "Hello everybody!" (*Children respond*) "I wanted to come by and bring you something." (*Hands Brady an envelope*)

BBB: "Oh! Thank you!"

Babs: "I can't stay. I've got to get back to work. Lots of flowers to sniff, you know!"

BBB: "Oh yes! There are so many beautiful large fields of flowers this time of year!"

Babs: "You're quite right! And you know how much I love my work!"

BBB: "I do indeed!"

Babs: "Just the other day I was over on the other side of that enormous valley!"

BBB: "Oh yes!"

Babs: "You know the one I mean!"

BBB: "Of course! It's one of my favorites!"

Babs: "Yes. I know. Oh my! Listen to me! There I go! Talking on and on when I have so much to do."

BBB: "That's all right. You know I always enjoy your company."

Babs: "Thank you. But I must go! When you get a chance, look inside the envelope."

BBB: "I will. Thank you again for bringing it by."

Babs: "You're welcome." (*Waves Goodbye*) "Goodbye everybody!" (*Children respond*).

BBB: (*Looks at envelope*) "Another surprise! What a fun day!" (*Children respond*) "I'd better see what it is." (*Looks inside, pulls out a letter*) "It's a letter. Do you get letters? (*Children respond*) "Do you ever write letters?" (Paul enters; Holding a scroll and writing pen; He sits) "Well, maybe you don't now, but you will when you learn how to write! In the Bible, the Disciple Paul wrote many letters to tell the other Disciples how to work and teach the people in the church. He wrote a letter that talked about prayer too! Watch this!"

Scene III

Paul/Timothy: *(Paul writes a letter to his friend Timothy. Runner enters. Paul hands letter to him. Runner exits. Timothy enters down right. Church members enter. Runner enters. Gives letter to Timothy. Timothy reads letter to congregants as Paul speaks the same words)* "Do good...! Be kind to each other. Be happy, thankful! And Always Pray!' That's what God wants us to do!"
                    (1Thessalonians 5: 16-17)

(Paul, Timothy and Congregants Exit)

BBB: *(To Children)* "Yes! Paul wrote many letters to the Disciples telling them how to help the people. And he always reminded them how important it is to pray. That was a good lesson wasn't it?" *(Children Respond)* "Remember that God wants us to pray. Here's a song that tells us to pray."

Song: Pray Pray Pray (Brady Sings)

END

APPENDIX

SONGS

Sue L. Adkins

THREE CHILDREN'S BIBLE PLAYS
By Sue L. Adkins

Music and Lyrics Written By Sue L. Adkins
(Printed Song Lyrics)

Songs

"Tell The Truth"

1. Let's Learn
2. Tell The Truth

"Jesus In The Temple"

3. OBEY
4. You Must Obey
5. The Bible

"Pray"

6. What Do You Do When You Pray
7. When You Pray
8. Pray Pray Pray

CHILDREN'S BIBLE PLAY SONGS

LET'S LEARN
MUSIC AND LYRICS BY SUE L. ADKINS

(CHORUS)
WE'RE GONNA' LEARN
YES LEARN
PLAY
HAVE SOME FUN
PRAY TRUST AND OBEY
SO COME ALONG
AND LISTEN CLOSE
TO WHAT WE HAVE TO SAY

(CHORUS)
WE'RE GONNA
LEARN
YES LEARN
PLAY
HAVE BIG FUN
PRAY

Sue L. Adkins

TRUST AND OBEY
NOW COME ALONG
AND LISTEN CLOSE
HERE'S WHAT WE HAVE TO SAY

VERSE;
LEARN
WAIT YOUR TURN
DON'T FIGHT
DO RIGHT
PRAY TRUST AND OBEY
BELIEVE ACHIEVE
YOU WILL RECEIVE
HERE WHAT WE HAVE TO SAY

VERSE:
WORK
MOVE AND TRY
COME ON COMPLY
TRUST PRAY AND OBEY
I'LL TELL YOU WHY
NOW DON'T BE SHY
HERE'S WHAT WE HAVE TO SAY

(CHORUS)
WE'RE GONNA
LEARN
YES LEARN
PLAY HAVE BIG FUN
TRUST
PRAY AND OBEY

42

NOW COME ALONG
AND LISTEN CLOSE
HERE'S WHAT WE HAVE TO SAY

BRIDGE:
A PERFECT PLAN
BELIEVE YOU CAN
A USEFUL TOOL
AND IT'S REAL COOL

VERSE:
STORIES TO TELL
THINGS GO SO WELL
NOW TAKE YOUR TURN
COME ON LET'S LEARN

(CHORUS)

Sue L. Adkins

TELL THE TRUTH
MUSIC AND LYRICS BY SUE L. ADKINS

(CHORUS)
TELL THE TRUTH
GROWNUPS AND YOUTH
DO WHAT'S RIGHT
BOTH DAY AND NIGHT
OH YOU BEE
A GOOD BEE
AND TELL THE TRUTH

VERSE:
JESUS SHOWS
HOW WE SHOULD BEE
THERE ARE LESSONS
FOR US TO SEE
YOU BEE
A GOOD BEE
TELL THE TRUTH
YOU BEE
A GOOD BEE
AND TELL THE TRUTH

BRIDGE:
TRUTH
MEANS YOU DON'T

HAVE TO MAKE UP A STORY
OF SOMETHING THAT HAPPENED
SO BAD, WRONG, OR GORY

IT MAKES THINGS EASY
YOU DON'T HAVE TO STRAIN
COME UP WITH AN ANSWER
JUST KEEP THINGS PLAIN

(CHORUS)

OBEY

MUSIC AND LYRICS BY SUE L. ADKINS

VERSE:
DO YOUR BEST
OBEY
EACH AND EVERY DAY
JESUS SAYS WE SHOULD
AT HOME, AT SCHOOL
AND PLAY
IT'S NOT ALWAYS EASY
TO DO WHAT'S RIGHT
BUT WE'LL TRY
WITH ALL OUR MIGHT

VERSE:
OBEY MOM AND DAD
AND YOUR TEACHER TOO
IT SAYS IN THE BIBLE
JUST WHAT WE
SHOULD DO
SOMETIMES IT SEEMS HARD
TO DO WHAT'S RIGHT
COME ON TRY
YOU'LL WIN THE FIGHT

(CHORUS)
YOU MUST OBEY
YOU MUST OBEY
EVERYDAY
YES! THAT'S THE WAY
AND THROUGH IT'S NOT EASY
SOMETIMES IT SEEMS HARD
NO IT'S NOT EASY
TO DO WHAT'S RIGHT
BUT TRY
WITH ALL YOUR MIGHT

BRIDGE:
YES! IT'S OKAY
DO RIGHT! OBEY
TRY! WORK AND PLAY
OUR PARENTS SAY
KIDS SHOULD OBEY
BOTH NIGHT AND DAY
A BRIGHTER DAY
IS ON THE WAY

VERSE:
IT'S NOT ALWAYS EASY
SOMETIMES IT'S REAL HARD
YOU TRY AND YOU TRY
NOT TO LET DOWN YOUR GARD
BE STEADFAST
BELIEVE
WITH ALL YOUR HEART
LET GOD LEAD YOU

HE'S THERE FROM THE START

(CHORUS)
YOU MUST OBEY
YOU MUST OBEY
EVERYDAY
YES! THAT'S THE WAY
AND THOUGHT IT'S NOT ALWAYS EASY
SOMETIMES IT SEEMS HARD
NO! IT'S NOT ALWAYS EASY
TO DO WHAT'S RIGHT
BUT TRY
COME ON TRY
YOU'LL WIN THE FIGHT

YOU MUST OBEY
MUSIC AND LYRICS BY SUE L. ADKINS

VERSE:
YOU HAVE A JOB TO DO
WHEN MOTHER TELLS YOU TO
PICK UP YOUR TOYS
CAN'T YOU
ALWAYS OBEY

VERSE:
GOD LOVES YOU
AND COMMANDS
OBEY YOUR PARENTS AND
A SLIP UP NOW AND THEN
HE'LL UNDERSTAND

(CHORUS)
OBEY YOUR MOTHER
OBEY YOUR FATHER
TRUST IN GOD
FOR THERE'S NO OTHER
TRUST GOD AND DO HIS WILL
HE LOVES YOU SO AND STILL
COME ON GET WITH THE DRILL
YOU MUST OBEY

BRIDGE:
MOTHERS LOVE THE WAY
YOU DO WHAT THEY SAY
EAT WHAT YOU'RE FED
MAKE UP YOUR BED

GO WHERE YOU'RE LED
NOW REST YOUR HEAD
PICK UP YOUR TOYS
(OBEY) GIRLS AND BOYS

VERSE:
TRUST GOD AND DO HIS WILL
HE LOVES YOU SO AND STILL
COME ON
GET WITH THE DRILL
YOU MUST OBEY

(CHORUS)
OBEY YOUR MOTHER
OBEY YOUR FATHER
TRUST IN GOD
FOR THERE'S NO OTHER
TRUST GOD AND DO HIS WILL
HE LOVES YOU SO AND STILL
COME ON GET WITH THE DRILL
YOU MUST OBEY

THE BIBLE
MUSIC AND LYRICS BY SUE L. ADKINS

(CHORUS)
BIBLE
THE BIBLE
STUDY IN THE BIBLE
READ IT NOW
TO FIND OUT HOW
THEY ALL GOT SEPARATED
(THEY) LOOKED AND LOOKED
FOR THEIR SON
SADNESS IT CREATED
BIBLE
BIBLE
ITS ALL IN THE BIBLE
READ IT TODAY
SOON
RIGHT AWAY
TO TEACH YOU WHAT TO DO AND SAY

VERSE:
JOURNEYED TO JERUSALEM
EARLY ON THAT DAY
WALKED MILES AND MILES
TO THAT CITY
FAR AWAY

VERSE:
ALONG THE MARKET WAYS
ARE COLORFUL DISPLAYS
SETUP ALL AROUND
BRIGHT SIGHTS AND SOUNDS

VERSE:
SOME LOOK, GAWK AND STRAY
WENT THEIR SEPARATE WAY
BRIGHT POTS OF CLAY
BUT HE GOT LOST THAT DAY

VERSE:
WENT THIS WAY AND THAT
WARES SET OUT ON MATS
THINGS ALL AROUND
THEIR SON COULD NOT BE FOUND

(CHORUS)
BIBLE
THE BIBLE
STUDY THE BIBLE
READ IT NOW
FIND OUT HOW
THEY GOT SEPARATED
(THEY) LOOKED AND LOOKED
FOR THEIR SON
WHAT SADNESS

IT CREATED
BIBLE
THE BIBLE
ITS ALL IN THE BIBLE
READ IT TODAY
SOON
RIGHT AWAY
TO TEACH YOU WHAT TO DO AND SAY

Sue L. Adkins

WHAT DO YOU DO WHEN YOU PRAY
MUSIC AND LYRICS BY SUE L. ADKINS

(CHORUS)
YOU CAN TALK TO GOD
ANY TIME ANY PLACE
TELL HIM WHAT YOU WANT
TELL HIM WHAT YOU THINK
EVEN WHEN YOU'RE AT THE SKATING RINK

PRAY AT HOME
PRAY IN YOUR CAR
PRAY WHEN YOU'RE NEAR
AND WHEN YOU'RE FAR
TALK TO GOD
TALK TO GOD!

VERSE:
PRAY ANYWHERE
RIGHT WHERE YOU ARE
SAY WHAT YOU THINK
MAKE THAT LINK
FACE THINGS DON'T BLINK
GRAB HOLD DON'T SWRINK

(CHORUS)
YOU CAN TALK TO GOD

ANYTIME ANY PLACE
TELL HIM WHAT YOU WANT
TELL HIM WHAT YOU THINK
EVEN WHEN YOU'RE AT THE SKATING RINK
PRAY AT HOME
PRAY IN YOUR CAR
PRAY WHEN YOU'RE NEAR
AND WHEN YOU'RE FAR
TALK TO GOD
YES! TALK! TO! GOD!

Sue L. Adkins

WHEN YOU PRAY
MUSIC AND LYRICS BY SUE L. ADKINS

(CHORUS)
WHEN YOU PRAY
(YOU CAN) BOW YOUR HEAD
WHEN YOU PRAY
(YOU CAN) CLOSE YOUR EYES
WHEN YOU PRAY
(JUST) TALK TO GOD FROM YOUR HEART
WHEN YOU DO
THANK HIM TOO
HE GIVES GRACE
IT'S FREE
A FREE GIFT TO YOU

VERSE:
WHEN YOU PRAY
YOU CAN SAY
WHAT YOU HAVE
IN YOUR HEART
THINGS THAT HURT
AND THAT MAKE YOU SO SAD
IT WILL HELP
WHEN YOU DO
HE GIVES GRACE
IT'S FREE

A FREE GIFT TO YOU

VERSE:
WHEN YOU PRAY
YOU CAN ASK GOD
FOR HELP
FOR THE THINGS
YOU DID WRONG
AND YOU KNOW
ARE NOT RIGHT
WHEN YOU DO
TAKE HIS GRACE
REMEMBER TOO
TAKE HIS GRACE
IT'S HIS FREE
GIFT TO YOU

BRIDGE:
HE WILL HELP
AND FORGIVE
AND FORGIVE
HE GIVES GRACE
YES, HE GIVES GRACE
IT'S FREE
A FREE
YES, A FREE GIFT TO YOU

(CHORUS)
WHEN YOU PRAY
(YOU CAN BOW YOUR HEAD
WHEN YOU PRAY

Sue L. Adkins

(YOU CAN) CLOSE YOUR EYES
WHEN YOU PRAY
(JUST) TALK TO GOD FROM YOUR HEART
WHEN YOU DO
THANK HIM TOO
HE GIVES GRACE
IT'S FREE
YES A FREE GIFT TO YOU

PRAY PRAY PRAY
MUSIC AND LYRICS BY SUE L. ADKINS

(CHORUS)
PRAY PRAY PRAY
PRAY PRAY PRAY
WHEN YOU ARE SAD
COME ON AND
PRAY PRAY PRAY
PRAY PRAY PRAY
(EVEN) WHEN YOU GET MAD
YOU'VE GOT TO
PRAY PRAY PRAY
PRAY PRAY PRAY
WHEN THINGS GO BAD
TALK TO GOD
HE'LL GIVE A WINK OR NOD

(VERSE:)
CASTE TROUBLES AWAY
FEAR, DOUBT, WON'T STAY
BLUE SKIES NEVER GRAY
TO PRAY IS OKAY

(VERSE)
CLEAR YOUR MIND
LEAVE THE MESS BEHIND

PRAY AND
DO YOUR BEST
HE WILL DO THE REST

(BRIDGE:)
PRAY…
EVERY DAY
PRAY…
HEAR WHAT I SAY
PRAY, TRY
YOUR OWN WAY

(REPEAT CHORUS
(EVERYBODY SHOULD…)

THREE ONE ACT CHILDREN BIBLE PLAYS
BY SUE L. ADKINS

WITH MUSIC AND LYRICS
BY SUE L. ADKINS

Production Notes

All three plays are geared toward the pre-school audience, two and a half through five years old (2 ½ - 5). Each play is introduced by the character "Brady Bible Bumble Bee. Bumble Bee can be an older boy or girl, or an adult. (You can use the name "Bridget for a girl," or another of your choice. The Director has casting decisions. Consider the maturity level of character choices.

Characters:

"Tell The Truth"

Brady Bible Bumble Bee, or Bridget (if a girl)
Man, Man I, II, III
Blind Man
Neighbor (leads Blind man)
Disciples I – III (Can be two or more player,
depending on number of participant available)
Jesus
Neighbor

"Jesus In The Temple"

Brady Bible Bumble Bee
Joseph
Bieleum
Travelers – six or more adults or older children
Teachers I – IV (Can be 1 – 6 players)
Snake Charmer
Vendors   (3 – 6 players)
Temple Teachers – (3 or more players)

"Pray"

Brady Bible Bumble Bee
Jesus
Disciples (3 – 6 or more players)
Babs Butterfly
Paul

Timothy
Runner (Mesenger)
Church Leaders (3 or more players)

Props:

"Tell The Truth"

Rope with hand-printed sign attached. Sign reads:
"TRUTH"
Worn Cloth Bag to hold Blind Man's Coins
Placards – letters "T", "R", "U" "T" "H" and sign
that reads "TRUTH"

"Jesus In The Temple"

Bell
Large Bag
Large Binoculars
Straw Baskets

Rubber Snake
Cloth, Baskets, Fruit
Juggler – Scarves
Big Book – with word "BIBLE"
Large Colorful Glasses
Large Book Mark

"Pray"

Large Bowl
Silk Sunflowers or some other bright flower
Large Mixing Spoon
Large Bag to hold items
Large placard w/word "Pray" printed in large letters'
Sound/Telephone Ring
Gift wrapped box
Letter (Envelope with letter inside)
Optional – Animal Skins bags – for water canteen

Costumes:

Brady Bible Bumble Bee – Bee Costume
Babs – Butterfly Costume
Biblical Period Costumes

Sue L. Adkins

Sue L. Adkins writes fiction and children's plays and books. She lives with her family in Plano Texas and works with her church, bringing productions of her work and the work of other writers to the congregation. Sue shares a message of hope and enlightenment in this text through lessons of positive Christian experiences. She encourages groups and organizations to perform and enjoy this work.

Sue presents three one-act plays to be performed by elementary through high school children. All three plays are geared toward the pre-school audience, two and a half through five years old (2 ½ - 5). Each play is introduced by the character "Brady Bible Bumble Bee. The plays teach valuable lessons on (1) telling the truth, (2) obeying, and (3) the power of prayer.

Cheudi Publishing, Plano, Texas 75094-0572

www.ingramcontent.com/pod-product-compliance
Lightning Source LLC
Chambersburg PA
CBHW060428050426
42449CB00009B/2182